HEROIC DOGS

True Stories of Incredible Courage and Unconditional Love from Man's Best Friend

Volume 2

Lou Jefferson

Copyrights

All rights reserved. © Lou Jefferson and Maplewood Publishing No part of this publication or the information in it may be quoted from or reproduced in any form by means such as printing, scanning, photocopying, or otherwise without prior written permission of the copyright holder.

Disclaimer and Terms of Use

Effort has been made to ensure that the information in this book is accurate and complete. However, the author and the publisher do not warrant the accuracy of the information, text, and graphics contained within the book due to the rapidly changing nature of science, research, known and unknown facts, and internet. The author and the publisher do not hold any responsibility for errors, omissions, or contrary interpretation of the subject matter herein. This book is presented solely for motivational and informational purposes only. The publisher and author of this book does not control or direct users' actions and are not responsible for the information or content shared, harm and/or action of the book readers. The presentation of the information is without contract or any type of guarantee assurance. This book is not meant to be used, nor should it be used, to diagnose or treat any medical condition. For diagnosis or treatment of any medical problem, consult your own physician. The publisher and author are not responsible for any specific health or allergy needs that may require medical supervision and are not liable for any damages or negative consequences from any treatment, action, application or preparation, to any person reading or following the information in this book. References, if any, are provided for informational purposes only and do not constitute endorsement of any websites or other sources. Readers should be aware that the websites listed in this book, if any, may change.

ISBN: 978-1537249568

Printed in the United States

Contents

Introduction 1
Katrina: Hurricane Katrina Savior 19
Eve: Fearless Rottweiler Saves Paraplegic from Burning Truck 25
Ginny: Breaking Boundaries and Saving Feline Lives 29
Trakr: Finder of the Last Survivor of September 11, 2001 33
Belle: Making Calls to Save a Life 39
Duke: Most Loyal Babysitter 43
Noah: Canine Shield and Life Saver 47
Treo: Decorated War Hero 51
Kiko: The Canine Surgeon 55
Yogi Saves the Day after a Tragic Bike Accident 59
Xena: Shelter Dog Brings Life to Autistic Boy 63
Toby: Heimlich Miracle 69
Parting Words 72
Other Books by Lou Jefferson 75

Introduction

We can begin this book with the question, "what is a dog?" Depending on whom you ask, the answer is likely to be quite different. Some people view dogs only as pets that require care but also contribute some companionship. Then there are others who are simply not dog people, who probably wouldn't give much thought to the question or answer at all. And then there are the people who really know what a dog is. These are the people whose lives have been touched in some way by a member of the canine family. They will tell you with certainty in their voice, that a dog is truly man's best friend, a companion capable of the greatest unconditional love, loyalty, and respect. Many people have extraordinary tales to tell of the special animals in their lives. Here in this book, we feature just a sampling of some of the most extraordinary tales of animal devotion, bravery, and love for mankind.

The relationship between man and beast is one that has been studied for decades, and the relationship between humans and canines has proved to be especially intriguing for researchers. There is a bond between us and dogs that is both unique and complex.

In the United States, more than half of all households are the home of at least one pet. And of these households, more than one-third have at least one dog.

As humans, we have an instinctual need to care for something. Even those people who might otherwise seem self-centered or callous often still have an urge to love and care for another living thing. Given how difficult human relationships can be at times, and how unsuited some people are for long term companionship, some of us look towards the animal world to help us fill that need. Even homes filled with love and care often still have a dog. Why? Because animal love is a different thing. Animal companions give us something unique that is difficult, if not impossible, to find in human to human relationships. They give us social support, filling some of our basic needs for companionship and attention, and comfort. How do you feel when you are around a beloved pet? Why do you feel this way? Just being around animals, especially a devoted and loving pet, such as a dog, soothes and calms us. It can actually make us better people in our hearts, and sometimes even in our communities.

The stories in this book take the complex human-canine relationship and illustrate how blessed we are to have each other. Many people think of pets as being completely dependent upon us for their survival. They depend upon us to feed and shelter them. They depend upon us for both their physical and emotional needs, especially dogs, which have evolved from wild species that once preferred to roam free. We have taken the wildness and calmed and domesticated it to a point where these animals are now dependent upon us for the most basic of needs. But what we fail to look at when we think in these terms is the many ways in which we are dependent upon them.

In the beginning, dogs were domesticated not for being loving household pets, but instead for being companions in nature, trained to help hunt and protect. While we might not depend on dogs for hunting as much these days, those instincts have never left. You will find that in each of these stories, there is a strong tie to these primitive instincts – whether it is being able to find their way to get help, hunting down attackers or fiercely protecting their families with courage and love – the spirit of their ancestors live strong in each of these dogs. In addition to being heroes and saving lives, our canine counterparts also help to improve our moods, lower blood pressure, get us more exercise, reduce stress and reduce thoughts and feelings of loneliness and hopelessness. Even without the stories in this book, it is evident that dogs are heroes who silently save our lives every day.

The Awards

Dogs perform heroic deeds every day without any recognition at all. Some of them are shown gratitude from the people whose lives they impact, while sadly, some are unrecognized altogether. There are however, several organizations that take the honoring of hero animals seriously. Many of the dogs in this book were honored for their actions. Following is just a sampling of the prestigious honors granted to some of our hero dogs.

Animal Hero Awards

Sponsored by the UK's Royal Society for the Prevention of Cruelty to Animals and the Daily Mirror, these awards are presented annually to the "most inspiring examples of bravery, dedication and resilience in the animal world" as stated on the foundation's website. Each award period they choose both members of the animal and human worlds to nominate for acts of courage and going above and beyond to protect the lives and well being of each other.

ASPCA Annual Humane Awards

Each year the American Society for the Prevention of Cruelty to Animals presents multiple awards to animals and people who demonstrate heroic behavior or who demonstrate incredible commitment to protecting the safety and well being of animals. There are several categories for these awards; they include: ASPCA Dog of the Year, ASPCA Cat of the Year, ASPCA Tommy P. Monahan Kid of the Year Award, ASPCA Public Service Award, ASPCA Henry Bergh Award, ASPCA Equine Welfare Award and the ASPCA Presidential Service Award.

The Dickin Medal

"For Gallantry" are the words that grace the bronze medal that signifies the highest level of honor for a military service animal. The ribbon's colors of green, brown and light blue stand for the naval, land, and air forces of the military. The medal was first awarded after World War II to honor the brave service animals who saved military and civilian lives. In the course of its existence, the medal has been awarded to sixty-seven animals, including thirty-one dogs, thirty-two pigeons, three horses, and one cat.

Genesis Award

Presented by the American Humane Society, this award is typically given to those with a strong media presence for their contributions in the awareness of animal rights and the prevention of animal cruelty. On occasion, this award is given for bravery to an animal who has shown exceptional courage and has contributed to the public knowledge of the value of animals worldwide.

Pet Hero Awards

Awarded by the Pet Philanthropy Circle, these honors are bestowed upon pets, individuals, business, and organizations that demonstrate and promote awareness of the causes associated with the protection of animals.

Stillman Award

Presented by the American Humane Association, this award is presented annually to animals who show extreme bravery and courage.

Various awards intended for humans

Possibly more remarkable than the recognition of any of the above awards is when a dog commits acts of such great courage and valor that his or her actions become recognized as being equal to or greater than those of human counterparts. There are a number of prestigious awards given to people annually that celebrate life and the courage to protect it. Many of the dogs mentioned herein are either the recipients of these awards or are honorably mentioned. This is just one fine example of how the human world and the canine world are so intimately intertwined. With bravery and respect we can protect and serve each other.

The Breeds

The inclusion of this section does not negate the fact that any dog, regardless of breed, has the capability of becoming a hero dog. The saddest stories of mixed breed shelter dogs from terrible beginnings can turn into the most triumphant of all hero tales. However, it is worth noting the top ten breeds for loyalty, service, and bravery. Many of the dogs in this book belong to one or more of the following breed families. Following is just a quick look at the most heroic of breeds, and devoted of pets, and what it is about them that make them such.

Golden retriever

Golden retrievers are the ultimate people dog. They are friendly, good with children, easy to train and are gentle enough that they are among the top choices for therapy dogs suitable to assist with a variety of physical and emotional conditions. Golden retrievers are naturally loyal and happy, but are also patient and intelligent, and they can easily pick up on subtle cues that others may miss.

Labrador retriever

This breed is one of the most popular breeds of pet dogs in the world. They have a mild temperament and are natural hunters and fetchers. Their devotion and ability to know exactly when and how to react in an emergency makes them among the number one contenders for dog hero status.

Collie

Most people have heard the story of Lassie, a fictitious account of a boy and his dog, in which Lassie almost always saves the day. This story really isn't far from the truth. Collies are naturally good with children, but also have a very keen sense of smell and intellect. Their delicate senses are able to detect the slightest change in the environment, including the physiology of a person. Collies also make excellent therapy dogs.

German shepherd

Bred to be aggressive working dogs, over the years this breed has developed a reputation for being fierce and unfriendly as family pets. One thing to remember is that while on one side there may be aggression, on the other side there is loyalty. Whenever an animal has a reputation for being too aggressive, we need to keep in mind that sometimes an aggressive animal is being protective of something or someone, and for the people who choose these breeds as pets, they may have picked this breed for this reason. They know with certainty that their pet will protect them at all costs. German shepherds are also known to have a very mellow, affectionate side to their nature, making them a good choice for families with young children, when guidance and training is used.

Beagle

Being somewhat smaller than many of their heroic counterparts, the beagle is often not the first breed that comes to mind when you think of dog heroes. But beagles were also bred to be a hunter's helper. This means they have an acute sense of smell and pay attention to the slightest of details. This, combined with their higher than average intelligence, makes them great choices for medical service dogs, especially for people with conditions that can be scented, such as diabetes.

Boxer

Bred to be powerful, big game hunters, the boxer can look fierce and intimidating. However, they are extremely loyal and protective by nature. This makes them an excellent choice for the job of family watchdog, keeping strangers and trespassers at bay. If you ever find yourself in an emergency situation, you can be sure that if a boxer ever leaves your side, it is only to further protect or serve you.

Rottweiler:

Another sweet dog with an undeserved reputation for being brutal. As a breed, this dog has in some cases been specifically bred for violence, but as a whole they are nothing but gentle and calm. Rottweilers are actually very mild tempered dogs that are easy to train. They, like most other hero dogs, are intensely loyal, so they will be at ease around family and on guard around strangers. Their purpose is to protect you. They are obedient, gentle with children, dependable, and always willing to work. They will stand by your side and defend, no matter what.

St. Bernard

This huge dog with an adorable face can be credited with saving countless lives of injured travelers, as they were used for search and rescue animals. Very resilient with incredible sense of smell, the St. Bernard is possibly the quintessential hero dog.

Schnauzer

This furry bearded creature is the picture of loyalty and steadfastness. Schnauzers are highly trainable and even tempered, meaning that in an emergency situation, they will come through as saviors of the day. They also enjoy a good game of fetch, making them perfect to have by your side if you are ever in an emergency situation where you need them to fetch help of any kind.

Bull Terrier

One of the most muscular and athletic of dog breeds, this beauty with an intimidating presence is actually quite mild tempered. They have extremely fine tuned reflexes making them quick to act. Combine this with their keen mental agility, and they make remarkably reliable companions. With loyalty and a strong protective instinct, the serious but good natured bull terrier will stand by your side no matter the circumstances.

The Heroes

Here we get to the heart of the matter; the canine heroes that have influenced, protected and saved the lives of humans. Although each of these stories is different, and each dog has a different personality, when you read about their acts of courage (all under varying circumstances), you will find that there are striking similarities between them all. All these dogs found a way to combine their natural instincts with how they have been taught to act in the human world. They all put the safety and security of another before their own, and each dog has forever won the hearts and gratitude of people around the world. There are no boundaries to the ways that these most loyal of companions are willing to stand up and protect. These loyal friends act out of instinct and devotion. Here we present twelve of the most remarkable hero dogs of modern times.

Katrina: Hurricane Katrina Savior

Many animals have a sixth sense, something deeper and more attuned than our own, that helps them survive during dire situations. It is not uncommon to hear of an animal alerting or otherwise helping their human companions during dangerous times. Some of these acts of courage are a little more heroic than others, but each forever leaves an imprint on the heart of the human. Occasionally, one of these animals will use their unique powers to help not only their human companions, which they consider to be their family, but also complete strangers with whom they have no emotional ties or feel connected to in any way. One such dog that sacrificed itself for the sake of an unknown human is a black Labrador named Katrina.

Hurricane Katrina was one of the deadliest natural disasters to ever affect North America. In late August of 2005, the tropical storm turned into a deadly and destructive category five hurricane as it hovered above the Gulf of Mexico. The storm retained its category five status as it ravaged the southeastern coastal areas from Florida to Texas, easing slightly as it came inland toward Louisiana, but still maintaining a category three status, leaving in its path destruction and devastation that, more than a decade later, has still not been fully rectified in some areas. In the New Orleans region of Louisiana, it was estimated that nearly eighty percent of the city and its structures were flooded, under water that would not relent for weeks. An evacuation order was put in for the city, and more than a million citizens were able to flee. However, not everyone was able to escape, and tens of thousands of people were left trapped in the underwater city, some able to seek shelter, while others were not so lucky. To date, there has still been no official death toll cited for the citizens of New Orleans during Hurricane Katrina, but the number is estimated to be at least 1,500. One man escaped his death at the hands of the storm, thanks to a dog we now call Katrina.

As search and rescue were scouring the area, looking for survivors, this brave dog risked her own life in order to save a man, who was quickly succumbing to the rising waters. Imagine yourself, holding on to anything you possibly could, waving your spare arm in an attempt to alert rescue workers of your location. The flood water brushing against you and soaking you completely as you frantically and urgently seek shelter and hope. This was the exact scenario for many of the people trapped within the flood ground of Louisiana, including the man whose life was saved by Katrina. She went on her own, without prompting, and pulled this man to higher ground, where he was not only free from the dangers of the water, but in a position where he was visible to rescue teams. While this one man has been the most vocal about Katrina's heroic acts, it is rumored that she actually saved many lives during the days and weeks following the storm. It is obvious that Katrina has the heart of a hero, but it becomes even more interesting when we stop to consider the nature of Labrador retrievers. Katrina, and her Labrador counterparts, have historically been known as helper and worker dogs, especially in the fishing industry, where they are very good at fetching things out of icy waters and hauling heavy, wet nets through the surf. Katrina, like other black labs, is a highly sensitive and intelligent dog who shows a general fondness for strangers. That day that she saved a man from drowning in the cold waters of Hurricane Katrina, she was instinctively tuned into the nature of her ancestors, battling cold waters and hauling precious cargo to dry land.

The following spring in 2006, Katrina received one of the highest honors when she was the recipient of the Humane Society of the United States' prestigious Genesis Award for bravery. The Genesis Award is granted annually and typically goes to those people in the news and entertainment industries for their contribution to the awareness of animal issues. That year, Katrina joined the ranks of celebrities as she accepted this well deserved tribute.

It is also worth mentioning that Katrina did not act alone during the rescue phase of Hurricane Katrina. Along with Katrina, other canine heroes worked to save human lives, including another well known Labrador hero named Jake. If it was possible to pay extended tribute to each of these animals it would surely be worth it. These dogs offered more than their bravery during the storm and its aftermath. They presented us with the chance to look at the canine world in a way we seldom get the opportunity to do. Some of the dog heroes of Hurricane Katrina were brought in to specifically be search and rescue dogs. These dogs were trained for such a disaster. However, so many of the search and rescue dogs were already there, simply defending their own territory, much like Katrina. They were there refusing to back down until the immediate sense of danger and peril had passed, until they were able to calm down their senses and quiet the inner voice that led them on in a need to save and protect not only their own, but all of the others in need around them.

In times like this, we think about the dangers to the human flood victims and the members of the emergency response units. Without a doubt, there is potential for harm – and fatalities – during any emergency relief effort of the scale that was Hurricane Katrina. But to the canine world, there is an entirely new set of potential hazards. While in some circumstances, Katrina and her fellow canine heroes are able to better navigate the treacherous environment, there were actually many conditions that would make a disaster such as Hurricane Katrina deadly for any animal hero. Consider the unpredictable temperature of the waters that flooded the area, or how the currents were affecting rescue efforts and people's ability to hold onto any dry perch that they could find. The weather was unpredictable, and the rising flood waters even more so. Katrina could have suffered any number of deadly outcomes by swimming out to bring others to safety. The destruction had left behind massive amounts of rubble, including sharp rock, broken glass and perilously perched heavy objects just waiting to topple with the next kiss of a windy gust. The scenario really demonstrates that fragility of both human and canine lives. The fact that we are able to recognize this also means that there are times that we might not be so brave, especially when faced with the possibility of our own mortality. Katrina had no such fear. She carried on in the face of tremendous challenges to save lives that were on the edge of being lost. Because of her, someone goes to bed tonight without shedding a tear for the loved one that they lost in the fateful storm that brought destruction to the entire region.

This story pays tribute the immense capacity of the canine spirit. Katrina, and the other dog heroes of Hurricane Katrina, saved lives that otherwise would have been lost, while bravely risking their own lives without thought. The pure instinct to protect and rescue is an admirable quality of our canine friends.

Eve: Fearless Rottweiler Saves Paraplegic from Burning Truck

If you, or anyone you know, is living with a debilitating disease or impairment, then you understand the challenges that come with the ordinary tasks of everyday life. Many of us, with no personal experience with such conditions, can only imagine the struggles – including the unexpected ones – that can arise from any situation. A woman named Kathie Vaughn knows very well that when your body is in some way compromised, what might seem like a minor problem at first can quickly escalate and threaten your life and safety. Kathie suffers from multiple sclerosis, which is a disease that affects the central nervous system. With multiple sclerosis, the immune system attacks the nerve fibers and the myelin sheaths that protect them. This causes damage and destruction of the nerve fibers and affects the ability of nerve impulses to travel from the brain to the spinal cord, resulting in a range of symptoms which can be mild or severe. Kathie is a paraplegic – paralyzed from the waist down – this loss of function in the limbs a natural progression of the disease.

Thanks to the service dog industry, people with disabilities are able to acquire steady and reliable animal companions to assist and protect them. Kathie's canine companion is a Rottweiler named Eve.

On one fateful day, Kathie purchased a truck that would enable her to drive herself around self sufficiently. It was just her and Eve in the truck that morning, as they traveled along the road. At one point in their journey something began to go wrong with the newly purchased vehicle. The back end of the truck began to fishtail, and in order to prevent losing control of the vehicle, Kathie brought the truck to a screeching stop. Imagine for a moment, not only the frustration of just purchasing a vehicle and immediately having mechanical issues, but also being in this situation and not being physically able to examine the problem. As if this weren't traumatic enough, things were about to get worse.

As Kathie and Eve were sitting in the cabin, Kathie considering their situation and deciding what to do next, the inside of the truck began to fill with smoke and fumes. The smoke was black and thick, and it was obvious that some part of the vehicle had caught on fire. Kathie thought quickly and first pushed Eve out of the truck. This was the perfect first move because if she had attempted to get out first, it would have been difficult for her to get back in to retrieve the dog. It was a move that would eventually save her life. Her next step was to try to reach her wheelchair, so she could get it out of the truck and eventually get into it so that she could escape the scene safely – except there was so much smoke she could not see or reach the wheels of her chair. The panic that would overcome anyone in this situation would be overwhelming, however through this disaster; Kathie had a clear thinking friend whose only concern was for Kathie's life. That friend was Eve.

Eve, recognizing that her companion was in serious danger, refused to leave her side. She understood that Kathie was unable to escape on her own. Eve used her mouth to grab Kathie by the ankle and drag her away from the truck. When they were just far enough away to escape possible death, the truck finally burst into flames. Some dogs might have felt that their owner was in a reasonably safe place and become skittish of the growing fire, but not Eve. She continued to fight for Kathie's life and brought her further away from the explosive flames towards a nearby ditch.

Soon after this, police began to arrive on the scene. The official knew that the way the flames were spreading that they soon would be reaching the gas tank, a situation that was incredibly dangerous for Kathie and Eve, even as far away as they were. Kathie used what strength she had left to try to move herself further away from the flames. The first responders were trying to control the situation and were yelling to Kathie that she must get further away. Kathie was slow, so Eve grabbed onto her and dragged her dozens more feet to safety.

Once they were a safe distance away from the vehicle, Kathie and Eve watched together as the truck was consumed in flames. Eve sitting dutifully at her side, Kathie's mind was no doubt racing, thinking of all of the possibilities, and feeling gratitude for the friend sitting at her side. There are many people with disabilities who are fortunate to have the aid of a helper service dog. These dogs are specially trained to know how to react in a variety of everyday and emergency scenarios. Even with this, what are the chances that a service dog would be trained to pull its owner away from a truck on the verge of bursting into flames? One has to think that Eve's reaction was part training, and part pure intuition, combined with love.

Rottweilers are no strangers to negative press and prejudice based on stories of unpredictable and extreme aggression. It is true that some dogs of this breed are overly aggressive, as is true with almost any dog breed.

It is also true that a Rottweiler can be the most trustworthy and protective companion that a person can have by their side, as we are sure Kathie would attest. Rottweilers by nature are sensible, serious, and reliable. They constantly take notice of their surroundings with quiet observation. They are strong, powerful, and confident. This confidence means that when they see the need for action, they act swiftly and continue until the task is met. If you were to say any of those things, let alone all of those things, about a human, and then tell the story about how they saved a paraplegic woman from a burning truck, you might consider them a superhero. In this case, the description is not far off. Eve is a true superhero, a warrior who risked her own life to save another.

After Eve saved Kathie's life she was awarded the American Humane Association's Stillman Award, a prestigious award (named after William Olin Stillman, one of the association's early presidents), for her unfaltering bravery in saving her companion's life. Eve is stellar example of the valor and respect deserved not only by herself but by her breed as a whole.

Ginny: Breaking Boundaries and Saving Feline Lives

You have likely heard the phrase "Fighting like cats and dogs". Canines and felines have a reputation for being natural enemies. Even when it comes to which to choose as a pet, you will often find that, aside from the people who are just animal lovers and adore them equally, dog people and cat people are quite different. It's not unusual to find, when you gather a cat and dog in the same place, a resulting combination of low growls and slithering hisses. As always though, there are exceptions to the rule. Some cats and dogs not only get along fine, some of them actually form bonded friendships. Even so, it takes a special kind of animal to always cross the bridge of differences. It takes an even more special animal to always seek out and help those of a different species that are in need. Ginny, the cat-saving dog, is one of those special creatures.

It is a classic story of someone coming from dire circumstances being able to rebuild their lives and help others. Except, in this case we are not talking about a person, we are talking about Ginny – a Siberian husky and schnauzer mixed breed dog. The story of Ginny's beginnings as a puppy are a mystery, but where her story does start is at a point that is tragic and tugs at your heart. Ginny was a mother, and by her side were three of her little puppies, when they were all found locked in the closet of a vacant apartment, abandoned without any water or nourishment for about a week. She was on the brink of death when she was found and the veterinarian she was taken to believed that her condition was beyond hope; that she would not survive. She was set to be euthanized when something changed the mind of the medical caregivers. They decided to wait, and give Ginny some more time. The strong willed and tender hearted canine managed to turn it around and survive. With her and her puppies returned to health, Ginny was given the chance for a new life. Unfortunately, there was not a family available to claim Ginny and her puppies, so they were then transferred to a local shelter to be put up for adoption.

There isn't a dog that enters a shelter that you don't wish for a happy ending for. If you have ever walked through an animal adoption facility, then you know that it is impossible to resist all of the faces, the way they all look at you with tender eyes, like each and every one is yearning to go home with you. It is hard to pick just one, and unfortunately in the end, not every dog will find a new forever home. However, for Ginny, there was a different fate in the plans. One day a man by the name of Philip wandered into the shelter and chose her, above all others, to be his new companion. Philip, suffering from depression, had been encouraged to adopt a special animal to help relieve the pain of his condition.

When he arrived at the shelter he was unable to adopt the dog that he had originally wanted, but the staff encouraged to spend a little time with Ginny. He was disappointed about not getting his original choice, but he agreed. It was in the brief minutes that he and Ginny spent together that he realized there was in fact something special, if even a little unusual about this canine, and it was that day that his life was enriched forever.

As he and Ginny began to spend time together as a family, developing the bond that forms between human and pet, he started to realize that Ginny had a unique talent – the talent for attracting, and being attracted to, feral cats, primarily those that were ill, injured, or otherwise in trouble.

There would be times that Philip and Ginny would be out for a walk, when she would dash off, with an air of determination. Something would catch her eye and she would paw or scratch until someone paid attention. The uncovered treasure was always a cat, or multiple cats, that needed attention. Whether it was saving a batch of stuck kittens or recognizing an injured cat in need, it is believed that in her lifetime Ginny saved the lives of over one thousand cats, even when doing so meant that she was putting herself in danger. While most dogs make a habit of either toying with, aggressively approaching, or just being annoyed by anything in the feline category, Ginny was crossing boundaries and showing interspecies love.

The pair shared their home with about twenty of the cats, and found homes for some of the others. Those they couldn't house themselves remained on the streets, but they were fed twice daily by Philip and Ginny.

Ginny lived to be seventeen years old. Simple math tells us that just with the feral cats that we are aware of that she saved, that she averaged approximately fifty-nine saved lives a year. We can only imagine how this number may be even higher when we take into account the lives she may have saved before she was adopted, and the lives of other animals besides cats that she positively impacted.

Part of the reason Ginny may have been so in touch with the needs of the injured and helpless could have been an overactive maternal instinct, but part of it might just have been an amplification of the natural traits of her breed mix. Siberian huskies are known to be very aware, intelligent and strong minded, and Schnauzers are protective guard dogs with keen intuition. Many dogs of similar breeds are natural hunters, which is a personality trait that is likely encouraged by many owners. Most natural hunters recognize when another animal is smaller, weaker and more fragile than themselves and they see the opportunity to prey. Ginny took her inborn talents and focused them in the opposite direction, using her instinct for finding what would be prey and using it to heal and save, rather than hunt and destroy.

Ginny lived a long and full life of service, worthy of recognition. She eventually passed away at the age of seventeen. If felines could talk, it is certain that they would speak up for the brave and loving soul that was Ginny. If there is a heaven for animals, Ginny is surely there enjoying the company of all creatures great and small, but especially the sweet purring and cuddles of cats and kittens. During her lifetime she achieved recognition for her life saving efforts by being named "Cat of the Year" from the Westchester Feline Club for her unyielding devotion and heroism to the lives of feral cats.

For his part, her owner Philip says that it was meant to be. He says that Ginny gave him a purpose in life, and she showed him how to heal by saving and caring for these vulnerable creatures.

Trakr: Finder of the Last Survivor of September 11, 2001

On September 11, 2001, America endured one of the most traumatic and devastating events in her history: the attacks on the World Trade Center in New York. Worldwide, people watched the destruction in horror, knowing that countless lives were in the process of being lost. It is often in the most difficult of times that the greatest heroes step forward, the ones who otherwise remain quietly in the shadows. One such hero who emerged from the tragedy that day was a German shepherd named Trakr.

Trakr was trained as a police dog, which made him perfect for search and rescue work after the attacks. The thing is, Trackr wasn't from the New York area – in fact, he was not even from the United States. Trackr was the police dog of Officer James Symington, and together they made their way to New York City from Nova Scotia after seeing the attacks and the following rescue efforts on television. There were other search and rescue dogs at the scene; however, Trackr made a special contribution. The morning after the attacks, on September 12, 2001, Trackr found a woman, Genelle Guzman, who would be known as the last of the twenty survivors who were buried beneath the remains of the towers. Imagine the shock, fear, and hopelessness that you might feel buried beneath over thirty feet of ruble. She was buried that deep, yet when Trakr reached this particular pile of rubble, he dug and unrelentingly made sure that rescue teams knew that there was someone under the seemingly impossible pile of destruction. It was Trakr's strong sense and intuitive power that made it so that Genelle, who was trapped beneath debris for more than an entire day, was able to survive the tragedy, rather than being another senseless victim. She was the last person to be found alive.

While Trakr is now most recognized for his search and rescue efforts of 9/11, he actually had quite a history prior to the event. Being retired from his job as a police dog, his daily life had once consisted of tasks that included taking down criminal drug operations, as well as performing other search and rescue tasks. Trakr was one of the many unknown police dogs that serve every day, making our world a safer place and assisting in finding the lost and injured.

One might think that upon returning home that Trakr would have been recognized as a local hero and celebrity, but instead there were actually negative consequences to Symington's actions. Symington had been on leave at the time, but the officials at the police department where he worked were not pleased with him for taking his police dog and contributing to the search and rescue efforts without authorization.

What many people don't know is that police dogs are often euthanized after their service to the department. Symington stood up against this and prevented the Trakr being euthanized at the end of his service, saving his life. And because he did this, Trackr was able to save lives, too.

Trakr did rise to a certain level of fame, as he was featured in popular media outlets such as Time Magazine, the CBS Early Show, and CNN, among others. Trakr demonstrated to the United States a sense of duty and loyalty during a time when it was feeling wounded. Trakr not only saved lives that day, but also helped to rebuild the spirits of so many who watched or were victims of what happened that day.

Trakr was one of many, many dogs who fearlessly searched the aftermath of 9/11 for survivors. The exact number of search and rescue dogs who assisted in the efforts is unknown. The number is expected to be in the hundreds, taking into account those who were registered search and rescue dogs, brave civilians who brought their own dogs to the streets, and canines whose natural instincts brought them to the grounds. We have made efforts to salute the well deserving human heroes of that day, but some of our animal heroes have gone unnoticed. The hundred of dogs who assisted with the search and rescue efforts are still making an impact on human lives and the aftermath of that day.

Along with the search and rescue dogs, veterinarians were also present during those days, keeping careful eyes on the dogs and their health, making sure they were not put into situations too dangerous or suffering from hunger or dehydration. All of these years later, some of those dogs are still being carefully looked after, not just for the sake of their own health, but for the survivors and heroes of the attacks. By following the canine helpers and keeping track of their lives, prevalence and rate of disease and overall emotional well being, we are hopefully able to predict and treat similar conditions in the human victims and respondents. The information collected about the canine heroes of that day is still saving and protecting human lives, so in a sense, so are they.

As mentioned earlier, Trakr was a German shepherd, which is the most popular breed for police service dogs. German Shepherds are chosen for this line of work because of their general traits of intelligence, strength, natural tracking ability, endurance, and their ability to be taught skills combined with a sense of obedience. In recent years, there has been a decline in the number of German Shepherds being used for police work, because some breeders have worked to specifically breed out some of the traits that are so desired for it. Regardless of their reputation as law enforcers and helpers, German Shepherds, such as Trakr, will always remain among the most highly regarded of canine species.

The lifespan of a law service dog is sometimes shortened due to their line of work. The potential for injury and the contact with a variety of unfriendly substances can contribute to early disease and decline in health. At the age of 14, Trakr passed away due to complications of neurological disease, which may have been partly related to the service work that he did. However, before he passed away, Trakr was awarded the Extraordinary Service to Humanity Award. A few years after winning the award, Trakr once again entered the news after Symington won an essay contest with the prize being the opportunity to clone a pet, in this case, Trakr. After enduring some controversy, today there are five cloned offspring of Trakr, who were last known to be in the process of training to follow in Trakr's footsteps of being one of the unsung heroes of the service dog industry.

Belle: Making Calls to Save a Life

Have you ever looked at your canine companion and wondered if they know more about you than you do? There is a good chance the answer is yes. Certain dogs actually have the ability to detect abnormalities in human bodies. Police service dogs are able to detect when someone is under the influence of alcohol or drugs, and sense increased pulse rates and other signs of stress in potential criminals, and there are dogs who can detect conditions such as heart attacks, or even cancer. Some dogs are specially trained to detect subtle changes in the physiology of their owners. Belle, a beagle belonging to a man named Kevin Weaver, is one such dog, and her keen senses saved his life.

Kevin suffers from diabetes, which is a metabolic disease in which the body is unable to properly process food – specifically sugar. For people with diabetes, the body does not produce sufficient insulin to manage glucose in the body. This results in glucose building up and a consequent rise in blood sugars, or an equally dangerous situation when blood sugar is too low. This is usually due to improper amounts of medication, or poor nutrition. Living with diabetes requires constant monitoring and balancing. Achieving this balance can be difficult and must be taken seriously, as the complications of diabetes are a leading cause of death in the western world. Diabetes can be so serious for some people that they seek the assistance of service dogs trained to recognize the slightest difference in their physiology to help manage complications before they become life threatening.

Belle, being a medical service dog, was trained to be able to recognize changes in Kevin's blood sugar levels. Like other diabetes helper dogs, Belle had a very keen sense of smell that enabled her to detect changes in Kevin's physiology by the smell of his breath, or by licking his nose. She would do this periodically to check on him and alert him with her body movements when something was not right. On one particular day, Kevin's blood sugar had dropped to a dangerously low level. Low blood sugar, also called hypoglycemia, is an immediate medical emergency, as it can cause damage to the nervous system, coma, and even death. Kevin's had reached a very low level on that day. He collapsed and began suffering a seizure. Belle was able to recognize what was wrong with Kevin, and she knew he was unable to call for help himself. So, she did what anyone would do when someone was suffering a medical emergency. She dialed 911.

Because of the severity of Kevin's medical condition, the emergency number had been programmed into his phone and Belle had been trained to get the phone and dial the number using her teeth in case of just such an emergency. This is exactly what she did when Kevin collapsed. Belle was able to respond to Kevin's condition in a way that was calmer (and most likely faster) than if he had a human companion by his side during the episode. Thanks to Belle's keen sense and ability to recognize a dire situation, emergency responders were able to reach Kevin in time to save his life. Without her, there is a very good change that Kevin would not be here today.

Beagles make some of the best diabetes service dogs because of their natural hunter ability. They have one of the best senses of smell of all of the dog breeds, and can detect even the slightest deviation from what is normal. With a reputation for being scent hounds, beagles are also known for their family friendly demeanor which makes them excellent companions for families with younger children who suffer from diabetes.

As a result of her lifesaving actions, Belle was the first canine to be awarded the VITATM Wireless Samaritan Award, an award that is presented annually to the good Samaritans who use wireless technology to save lives, fight crime, and respond to other emergency situations. With so many people standing by with their phones, taking pictures of emergencies or dangerous situations, we could all learn a few things from Belle.

Duke: Most Loyal Babysitter

Babies and dogs have a few things in common. First of all, they show generous love and affection towards their parents. They are dependent upon you, but you are also in a way dependent upon them. They fill your heart with so much love and wonder that it is impossible to not love them fiercely and unconditionally. These commonalities are only part of the reason that people believe dogs and babies have a unique bond. Some people, especially those who are not intimately familiar with the nature of dogs, tend to become apprehensive when it comes to allowing dogs to intermingle with young children, out of fear that the animal will somehow hurt the child. However, most dog owners know that the reasons behind those fears couldn't be further from the truth. Yes, some dogs do have a disposition that doesn't mesh well with children; however the overwhelming majority of family dogs will be exceptionally welcoming to a new little human addition to the family, sometimes even taking the baby under its care and treating it as its own child.

One such dog who was protective of its new human sibling is a dog named Duke. What makes this story even a little more exceptional is that Duke breaks the misconception that it is mainly female dogs who act protectively over small children. Maybe this is because Duke came from what can be considered a broken family in the canine world. Duke was a shelter dog, waiting for a forever home, before he was adopted by the Brousseau family.

Six years prior to the birth of their daughter, the Brousseau family chose Duke, out of countless other choices, to be part of their family. According to a recorded interview, Duke was always a very obedient dog. For this reason the parents were immediately concerned about his erratic behavior the fateful night in 2012 when Duke would forever impact this family's life.

As many parents of newborn infants will tell you, it is incredibly difficult to put your baby down for a nap without constantly fretting about whether or not they are ok. How many parents have you heard say they feel the need to constantly check on their baby to make sure they are breathing, or feel that the age old advice of sleeping when the baby sleeps is impossible because although preciously peaceful, a sleeping baby is a source of anxiety for so many new parents. This is because most new parents know the risk of Sudden Infant Death Syndrome (SIDS) and the potential dangers of not taking certain precautions when caring for young babies. The absolutely terrifying aspect of this is that SIDS can strike without any warning at all. Most pediatricians will advise new parents to follow some practical advice and then suggest that if you follow all of the guidelines you should otherwise put these fears out of your mind, since the possibility of occurrence is actually quite low. Without any real known cause or certainty in prevention measures, most parents would give anything for a reliable monitoring system that would alert them at the first sign of any problem. There are several infant sleep monitors available on the market today, but after reading this story you might be inclined to believe there is no better monitor than a devoted, loyal pet. Any parent who has suffered the loss of a child would give anything for a second chance. A second chance is exactly what Duke gave the Brousseau family.

One evening they had put their sweet nine-week-old infant daughter down to sleep, like any other ordinary night. Imagine laying the most precious little head down, stroking her hair and inhaling the sweet scent of her skin before kissing her and leaving her there to peacefully slumber while you enjoy a little peace and quiet yourself. You finally manage to shut down all of the thoughts in your head and close your eyes, resting your own exhausted body when all of a sudden, your mild mannered, well behaved dog starts jumping on your bed, shaking and refusing to obey commands to calm down. This is what Duke did after visiting his sister in her room and realizing she had stopped breathing.

Alarmed by his erratic behavior, parental instinct kicked in and the parents decided to go in and check on their infant daughter. When they found her she was not responsive and not breathing. They immediately called emergency services, who were able to arrive quickly enough to save the baby's life.

There is no question that without the protective nature and instincts of Duke, the outcome of this situation would have been tragic rather than miraculous. Canines, such as Duke, have such a tremendous capacity for love and protection. Duke thought of this sweet baby as his own and protected her just as fiercely as a mama dog protecting her pups. He knew something was wrong, and he recognized the immediate need to alert the parents in order to save this sweet baby's life.

While animal shelters do the best they can to provide for animals in needs of homes, they are often stretched beyond their capacity. Some of the animals who come to them are in need of extra care and love, and each one is deserving of a new forever home. The sad truth is that many shelter animals never get the chance to find happiness and a second chance with a new family. Duke was one of the lucky ones, and there is a good chance he was able to recognize that his own life was saved the day he was adopted. The saving of a life is debt that can never truly be repaid. One can say Duke owes his family his life, but now they owe him something much larger, the life of one very precious little girl. Doctors were unable to determine the reason the baby had stopped breathing, but believe it may have been due to severe reflux. Regardless of the possible cause, it is hard to look at this situation and not think it was fate for Duke to find his home with this family. They are forever bonded, and forever grateful for each other.

Noah: Canine Shield and Life Saver

There are some horrors you hear about on the news and silently hope to yourself that you never have to endure such terror. Often, these events come straight from the local news. It seems all too common recently to hear of random assaults or aggression towards one another. The scariest of some of these involve senseless events such as road rage and random shootings. You can go through your days, taking extra care to not become involved in these tragedies, and doing everything you can to keep your family safe. Sometimes through a combination of the wrong place and the wrong time, you still might find yourself at the crossroads of disaster. If this ever happens, you can only hope to have a hero by side. A hero like a German shepherd named Noah.

When asked to think of the quintessential southern city, many people might say Atlanta, Georgia. The area is beautiful and abuzz with southern excitement, attitude, and flair. Of the people who live in the Atlanta area, many of them are filled with pride to call the area home. However, despite all that is wonderful about the region, according to neighborhood statistic reports, some neighborhoods in Atlanta and the surrounding areas rank rather poorly when it comes to violent crimes and general safety. Even when you take every precaution to keep your family safe, sometimes the most unfortunate of events can still happen. The story of Noah shows us just how fragile life can be and how things can change in the blink of an eye. In less time than it takes you to read this sentence, the lives of the Martin family were forever changed on the day after Thanksgiving in 2012.

Road rage, if you are not familiar, is defined as extreme and violent anger, while driving a motor vehicle, caused by someone's emotional response to difficult driving conditions. People experience road rage for a number of reasons, from other people driving erratically, to feeling as if your safety is in danger due to the driving habits of another, to simply being annoyed that other people are not driving as you would, or being caught up in extreme traffic. Lesser degrees of road rage are actually quite common. However, road rage sometimes extends beyond anger and annoyance, to the point when someone feels they must retaliate against another driver. What is very unusual is for someone to be the victim of road rage for a situation that they were not even involved in. The members of the Martin family experienced something that day which was against the odds, and truly terrifying.

The family were in their vehicle when they saw a road rage traffic altercation. Reports say the family themselves were not in any way involved in the situation that incited the road rage, but were simply witnesses. Even though the family were only bystanders, they were followed by the perpetrator to a strip mall. Reports say that several minutes later, the vehicle that followed them returned to the area, and began shooting at the vehicle and the family. Imagine the sheer terror you would feel if you suddenly found yourself, unprepared, in the middle of a battle zone. In spite of the terrible circumstances, there was one blessing on this day. Their dog, Noah, was in the car.

Before they were fully aware of what was happening, Noah forced himself between the oncoming bullets and the family members in the car, taking extra care to protect the children from the gunfire. The bullets that were fired entered the vehicle, one of them hitting Noah. Once the car had come to a stop, Noah managed to escape and continued protecting his family by chasing the shooters down the street in an attempt to catch them. Surveillance cameras of a nearby business caught the footage of a bloody and injured Noah, actively and aggressive pursuing the people who had threatened his family's life and safety. Unfortunately, Noah was so severely injured by the gunfire that he was unable to survive the extent of his wounds. Not only did Noah protect his family, he spent his final minutes of life trying to track down the people who dared to threaten the lives of the people he was devoted to.

Noah isn't the only animal who has taken a bullet to save a family member. It is interesting to discover that when you hear about dogs who are willing to jump into the line of fire to save their human companions, they are almost always of breeds that are viewed as overly aggressive and potentially dangerous as family pets. German shepherds, Rottweilers and bullmastiffs are the headliners in these stories of bravery. While most dogs will show some protective instincts towards their human family, some breeds were specifically bred over generations to protect and defend their territory, which includes their human family. Many breeds of dogs that have a reputation for being unfriendly are actually on the list of top family guard dogs. This is important to know, because the bad reputations of some of these breeds have led to mistreatment, abandonment, and even senseless killings. Knowledge and understanding of how each of these breeds responds and interacts is essential to protecting the animals who fiercely protect us.

While our favorite dog hero stories often involve happy endings for everyone, Noah ranks among those canines deserving the most special place in our hearts. The Martin family didn't deserve to be attacked under a storm of gunfire, they didn't deserve to have their lives threatened that day, and they didn't deserve to lose their most faithful companion to such senseless violence. Even with all this tragedy, we can look into the special part of our human spirit that recognizes the blessings in even the most tragic of situations. It is very likely that the Martin family would have lost at least one person that day, were it not for Noah's intervention. They have their lives because of the fierce bravery and loyalty of one very special German shepherd. This story reminds us to be present in the moment and appreciate all that we have, because we never know when our lives might change in an instant. Noah fought for his family to have many more moments together. He sacrificed himself and he fought through the pain of terminal wounds to protect and serve in the name of what is right and good, just like any true hero. Canine heroes are no less than human heroes, and in some cases, dogs have us beat in bravery and perseverance. With so much love and respect, dogs like Noah are remembered and honored every day by the people whose lives they have touched, and even saved.

Treo: Decorated War Hero

What would you consider the most dangerous job in the world? What would you consider the most respectable job in the world? What if you combined the two? If your mind is wandering towards the men and women who protect and serve their countries as members of the military, then we are thinking along the same lines. There are few positions that immediately bring to mind such respect and honor as those who serve. There is no question that these jobs come with tremendous sacrifice and little tangible reward. When we take a moment to give thanks to those who serve and protect, we should also keep in mind some of the unknown heroes and protectors of safety and liberty. Some members of the military didn't sign themselves up, but were instead offered because they showed themselves to be something special. I am speaking here of military dogs.

There have been military dogs for centuries. In the United States, military dogs have been used in every major combat, but were not officially recognized until World War II. In terms of history, this major world war, fought between the years of 1939 and 1945, is relatively recent. Before and since then, canine war heroes have been ever present on the scene, using their innate, natural powers and instincts to help save the lives of soldiers and civilians. Currently there are an estimated twenty-five hundred dogs serving in the armed forces, but this is only about half the dogs who enter the specialized training program, which focuses on physical prowess, the ability to detect weapons, bombs, and drugs and knowing when to attack an enemy.

Not every dog is cut out for military training. Some are specifically chosen for their unique abilities, while others are donated in hopes that they can fulfill some need and discover a purpose in life that they were unable to find as household pets. A Labrador named Treo was one of those animals donated to the armed services, in hopes that his slightly aggressive demeanor could be of service. He came to his training with only the background of being a misbehaving puppy, a little too aggressive and boisterous for family life. He would soon be trained, and would become one of the most effective and highly decorated military dogs in history.

Once Treo completed his training he was assigned to the The Royal Irish Regiment, where he and his handler, Sgt. Dave Heyhoe met for the first time. According to Sgt. Heyhoe, it was love at first sight between him and Treo, and it wasn't long before Treo became a valuable member of the platoon. One might wonder why with modern technology and increasing capabilities, it is necessary to bring along a cumbersome animal to some of the world's most dangerous and covert missions. The answer is very simple. To this day, the natural instincts of dogs like Theo more often than not surpass even the most advanced technology in their given skill set. In addition to this, technology means equipment. And equipment often requires a power source or elaborate set up and take down. The needs of a dog are far simpler, requiring only the same basic needs as their human comrades.

Treo was stationed in Afghanistan, where he was put to work sniffing out explosives. Word has it that Treo was like a living, breathing metal detector. No matter how many measures were taken to keep the explosives from being discovered, Treo was able to use his senses to discover them, and in the process save countless lives.

Treo's rise to heroic fame came from the fact that he discovered a hidden daisy chain, which is a collection of explosives wired together, meant to cause large scale destruction, most often to traveling platoons. It is said that these networks of bombs were placed by the Taliban, which is a fundamentalist group whose militia took control of portions of Afghanistan in the mid 1990's. Since then the group has been associated with major terrorist incidents worldwide. Treo became known as a fighter of terrorism when he was able to find two of these deadly devices, making him the most successful bomb detecting dog at the time.

Treo's years of military service spanned from 2002 until 2009, when he officially retired and was relieved of his duties. In 2010, Treo was awarded the prestigious Dickin Medal, which is said to be the animal world's equivalent to the Victoria Cross. The Dickin Medal was instituted in 1943 by Maria Dickin as a way to honor the animal soldiers of World War II. It is awarded only to the animals that show the most bravery, devotion, and gallantry while on duty serving in a branch of the armed forces. In the animal world, there is arguably no higher honor than to be the recipient of the award and the medal that hangs from a striped ribbon of green, brown, and light blue.

In the past, after dogs like Treo had completed their military service, it was standard procedure to either abandon or euthanize the animal. The general mindset was that these dogs had no value outside of their service. They had been trained for a very specific skill set, including being able to attack aggressively when needed. Thinking that these animals would have no place in the civilian world they were put down, rather than offered a chance at a retired war veteran's lifestyle. In the year 2000, United States President Bill Clinton changed that by signing Robby's Law, which states that all retired military dogs who are suitable for adoption will be available for placement after their service years. Hundreds of military dogs have now been given the opportunity to go on and have carefree, enjoyable lives after their years of sacrifice in the armed services.

Treo himself was able to enjoy his years of retirement with Sgt. Heyhoe. The two remained close for years to come. At the age of fourteen, Treo passed away in the arms of his handler and forever friend, Dave. He was treated with the highest degree of respect in his passing and burial. Treo was buried with his Dickins Medal and a Union Jack, bringing the evidence of his bravery, devotion, and sacrifice with him into eternity.

Kiko: The Canine Surgeon

Imagine that you are home, in bed and blissfully slumbering away a couple of margaritas when suddenly you are awoken by the most excruciating pain. You sit up in bed and find yourself in absolute shock at the image of your toe, bitten off by who you thought was your faithful canine companion. Some might wonder and hope that it was all a nightmare, but for a man named Jerry it was very much a reality.

Kiko, a terrier, was Jerry's pet and the perpetrator of what many people would consider a vicious attack. It is safe to say that in any ordinary circumstance a dog that randomly bites off the toe of one of their family members is likely to be met with unfortunate consequences. However, at that moment there was no time to think about why Kiko bit the toe or what punishment might be in Kiko's future. In that moment, the only concern was to get Jerry to the hospital, where he would eventually have the remaining part of his toe removed, as soon as possible.

Once Jerry was at the hospital and being treated the doctors began to run routine tests and blood work. This is when they discovered that his blood sugar level was an extremely high five hundred and sixty. For reference, normal blood sugar levels can range anywhere from eighty to one hundred and twenty mg/dl. A blood sugar level over five hundred mg/dl typically only occurs in severe diabetics and is considered to be a medical emergency. Two major things can happen when blood sugar levels reach this range. The first is a condition called ketoacidosis. Ketoacidosis occurs when your body produces an abundance of acids called ketones. When the body doesn't make enough insulin, which is the problem in diabetics, there is excess blood glucose that cannot get into the cells. The cells are unable to produce the energy they need for basic function. To compensate, they begin to burn stored fat for their fuel source and as a result, produce the ketones. Once the point of ketoacidosis is reached, there is a possibility of the ketones poisoning the entire body. Complications of this include low potassium, which can impair heart and nerve function, along with swelling around the brain. Secondly, blood sugar at these levels can also cause hyperosmolar syndrome, a serious condition in which the blood can develop a consistency that is thick like syrup, which can lead to life threatening conditions such as heart attack, stroke, and coma. On this particular day, Jerry's undiagnosed diabetes was on the verge of killing him silently, and if it weren't for Kiko amputating his toe while he slept, there is no certainty that Jerry would have woke up ever again.

Jerry didn't know he was a severe diabetic, and Kiko was not a trained medical service dog. It turns out, not only did Jerry have diabetes, but he was also suffering from an infection in his foot that had been festering, untreated, for some time.

How is it that this terrier was able to identify and respond to a severe problem with his owner's health? Dogs, even those that are not trained to do so, have the keenest sense of smell and are able to detect changes in the scents of people around them that are brought on by physiological changes. Have you ever noticed that most dogs are attracted to wounds? They have a natural instinct to lick the wounds and might even pester a person suffering from a severe wound unrelentlesly until they are able to tend to the injured area. This is because dogs, with nearly four times the number of olfactory receptors as humans, are able to detect the smell of damaged and decaying tissue, as well as the subtle change in body odor that is often brought on by severe diabetes. Kiko was simply giving in to his canine instincts, and at the same time, saving Jerry's life. The toe had been infected for quite some time; Kiko's response was his way of healing the damaged appendage. This instinct is strong enough that Kiko is not even the only dog on record to amputate a body part of a family member with their teeth. There have been other medical reports of dogs nipping or biting severely infected body parts of their human family members, forcing them to seek immediate medical attention. Troubled as it may seem, this strange instinct has actually saved many human lives.

Kiko is a Jack Russell Terrier. Classic characteristics of this breed include being highly intelligent and energetic, with a keen sense of the smallest details, and skilled at hunting and digging.

Each type of dog is slightly different in temperament and abilities. It is always amazing to look at the unique characteristics of a dog in comparison to their heroic actions. In many cases, had it been a different dog, with a different personality, there is a chance that lives might have been lost rather than saved. Kiko was born with the ability to sniff out disease and to attack it, curiously digging at it until it no longer exists. Jerry's life was in peril when he lay down to sleep, his body secretly being attacked by an unknown disease and a severe infection. Kiko, without a doubt, saved Jerry's life. The amputation of a toe was quite the blessing in disguise, even if at the time it seemed like something out of a bad dream.

Yogi Saves the Day after a Tragic Bike Accident

Lake Travis sets the scene for a beautiful community in Texas. A bit north of Austin, the Lake Travis area has abundant coastal views, strikingly blue waters, and lush nature all around. This region is home to Paul Horton and his life saving golden retriever, Yogi.

You can picture it in your mind. It is a breathtakingly perfect Texas day. The air is warm, and the breeze is mild. It is the type of day that begs you to spend time outdoors. In an area such as Lake Travis, outdoor recreation is quite common. Between nature trails and water sports, it's easy to enjoy the great outdoors and remain active. That was exactly what Paul was doing the day he decided to take a bike ride, with Yogi trotting along beside him.

Unfortunate as it is, it is often from the simplest of daily activities that devastation occurs. It is also during these times when we can be the most grateful for canine heroes. They can take a devastating situation and save it from being a deadly one. During the course of Paul's bike ride, he hit a bump in the path and went flying from his bicycle – an avid cyclist's worst nightmare. In spite of all safety precautions, devastating accidents can happen, and sometimes the most you can hope for is to be spared serious injury. Sadly, this was not the case for Paul. When he landed he was knocked unconscious. Once he began to regain consciousness, he looked around and noticed a significant amount of blood. He immediately tried to move, but discovered he was unable to move his legs at all. The accident had left him paralyzed from the waist down, severely injured with no means of seeking help. That was when he looked up and noticed that his faithful Yogi was still by his side.

Imagine now being in Paul's position. You can't move, and while you are grateful to see your dog beside you, you also realize that this dog likely won't understand what you need or how to get it. Out of pure desperation and hope you begin talking to your dog, urging them to get help. This is exactly what Paul did. He urged Yogi to go home and get help, telling him to "go on, go home and get help". A dog who has never been trained in emergency rescue might not know exactly what was being asked of him, however Yogi defied those odds, and did just as Paul asked.

Yogi raced back home, where he encountered neighbors of Paul's, who were out on a leisurely walk. Yogi was characteristically a reliable, well behaved and good natured dog, so when he approached the neighbors and was acting erratically, they knew something was wrong. Yogi would go up to them and bark, then scurry away in the direction of where Paul had fallen. Then he would go back up to them and repeat the behavior. They got the message, and followed Yogi all the way back to where Paul was, and from there they were able to get him the emergency attention he required. For Paul and Yogi it was a true Lassie moment.

Yogi is a golden retriever, a dog that has a reputation as being one of the friendliest around and therefore is one of the top ten choices for household pets. It was a deviation from his naturally docile nature that made Paul's neighbors stop and pay attention to the signals that Yogi was giving that day. Originally bred to be duck hunters, golden retrievers have a keen instinct of direction and purpose. Yogi instinctively knew what his duty was that day, and he quickly found his way back home. He knew exactly how to interact with people in order to get them to take notice so he could lead them back to Paul. Golden retrievers are pack dogs and stick closely to their families, never doubting that they are an equal part of the family dynamics. It is safe to say that Paul feels the same way, and that Yogi will forever have a place in Paul's family and heart.

If it weren't for Yogi that day, there is a chance Paul may have died or that his injuries would have been even more severe. Paul never regained the use of his legs, and continues to have only partial function in his hands, but he lives each day knowing how fortunate he is that Yogi went along with him for his bike ride that day. Not one to let life's twists and turns get him down, Paul continues to live a very happy and active life, taking time to enjoy each and every day.

Yogi became a bit of celebrity as his story spread across the nation. He became so well known that the Humane Society awarded him their Valor Dog of the Year Award. This recognition is given annually to dogs who demonstrate extraordinary courage and resolve to help a person in need. Yogi will be forever recognized in their hall of fame for his extraordinary actions that day.

There is no question that there is something special about golden retrievers. This story illustrates so much about the special bond between this breed of dog and man. From their unique ability to communicate, to the highly recognized healing power of their love and companionship, a golden retriever like Yogi is a forever friend. Unfortunately, in the summer of 2015, Yogi was diagnosed with stomach cancer and was given a limited time to live. At last reports, Yogi was receiving the best of care to ensure that his final days on this Earth were as comfortable and filled with love as the lives of the people he touched with his spirit and bravery. There are few opportunities in life to find a friend as loyal and devoted as Yogi. He will forever live on in the spirit of bravery that he exhibited that one fateful day.

Xena: Shelter Dog Brings Life to Autistic Boy

Some of the most treasured stories of heroes are the ones where great odds were overcome. The story of Xena is a tale of great adversity being turned into great triumph. It all started one day in September of 2012 when a Staffordshire bull terrier was brought into the Dekalb County Animal Shelter. At the time, Xena was only about four months old, but the pain and neglect she had endured was more than anyone, or any dog, should have to endure in a lifetime. When Xena entered the shelter, she was a weighed a scant four pounds. She was incredibly emaciated and on the brink of death that day. It is said that during her early life she was caged and neglected without proper food or water until one day she was dumped into someone's yard. The day that Xena made it to the animal shelter was a fateful one, not only for her, but also for one autistic eight-year-old boy.

When Xena was first examined, it was doubtful that she was going to survive. Her neglect had put her in a medical state that seemed nearly impossible to overcome. However, the people at the animal shelter did not give up on Xena. They began to treat her and she responded well to offers of food and water. She began to win over the hearts of all of those at the shelter as each day she gained a little more strength. One of the shelter employees decided to bring Xena home and continue her care there until she was fully healed. It was there that Xena gained her nickname "Xena, the Warrior Puppy". With the love and care of the shelter workers, Xena fully regained her health and was soon looking for a forever home with a family that would love and treat her as she truly deserved.

One day a family, the Hickeys, walked into the shelter, looking to adopt a dog. One member of the Hickey family was an eight-year-old boy who was autistic. Autism is a condition with a wide range of symptoms varying from mild and not very noticeable, to severe enough to impact daily living. Most people who are diagnosed with autism display some degree of difficulty with social interactions. This can present itself in several ways, from having difficulty with language pragmatics, which can impact communication, to not being able to handle the sensory input that is involved in social interactions. Many cases of autism are first diagnosed in the toddler or early education years, when parents or caregivers may notice a change in social behavior, mood, or even a loss of previously gained skills. Adjusting to a life with autism can be difficult for a family, and even with the help of trained professionals and therapies, it can be difficult for children and adults with autism to intermingle with their peers and society.

This was the case for the young autistic member of the Hickey family. While he had verbal communication skills, his world was shrinking rather than growing. At such a young age he was become more and more introverted, living in a world of isolation and closing off those that were around him. The family had been following Xena's story and had been awaiting the day when the shelter announced that she was available for adoption. Even though they had already fallen in love with her, even before she became part of their family, they never could have guessed the impact that Xena was about to have on their lives. As soon as Xena and the boy met later on their first trial day, you could almost see the sunshine burst within the boy's heart. They seemed to recognize each other, or at least that they each had a need only the other could fulfill, and they were both open to the possibilities of how they could change each other's lives. There was an instant bond and instant unconditional love.

There has been research conducted recently about the therapeutic use of animals in the treatment of autism. Findings have shown that autistic children who are around animals, especially those they have an emotional connection to, are more likely to develop certain social skills, such as the ability and willingness to keep and maintain eye contact, engage in social conversation (if somewhat limited) and show signs of joy. The young boy who became Xena's best friend not only confirmed these research findings, but exceeded any expectations.

Soon, he started to come out of his shell. He began using his well developed language skills and interacting with people, as opposed to disappearing into an isolated darkness, which was the path he was on before Xena entered their lives. Through their friendship, each day he became more and more open and interactive. His mother claims that of all the money she spent on therapy for her son, that Xena was by far the best therapy money could ever have bought. He, like other autistic children who have been given the opportunity to grow through the presence of therapeutic animals, has had the chance to better learn how to interact with others in society, and also better tolerate the simple and complex tasks of daily living.

There are many therapeutic service animals who help people with autism, as well as many other conditions and disabilities. These animals work daily to help and heal the people they work with. So, one might wonder what is so special about Xena. First of all, each service animal deserves recognition as being an unsung hero. But secondly, many service animals are handpicked based on breed or personality traits. Xena had a couple of strikes against her as a choice for a therapy dog. Being a bull terrier, the breed's reputation often precedes her. Many people who do not understand the breed consider them to be too aggressive, territorial, and sometimes too impulsive to be well suited for therapeutic use. Combine the terrible neglect and abuse the Xena endured as a young puppy and you might expect to find a dog incapable of expressing or receiving trust or love. This was not the case for Xena. Though her body was abused and neglected, her spirit was still intact. All she needed was for someone to love her, take care of her, and be trustworthy. It turns out there was a little boy out there who needed the same things from her in order to learn how to live in a world that expanded beyond the confines of his comfortable home.

To honor her journey and her remarkable spirit, the American Society for the Prevention of Cruelty to Animals awarded Xena with their Dog of the Year Award. Dressed up in her special sash and sparkling tiara, Xena looked as beautiful outside as she is inside. Xena is now a healthy adult dog, weighing more than forty pounds – more than ten times what she weighed when she was first brought to the shelter. Xena is also a major presence on media sites such as facebook, where she has a page devoted entirely to her and the awareness of animal cruelty and autism, two causes that are extremely close to this canine's heart.

Toby: Heimlich Miracle

Every so often on television, a program will show a scene where the actors are in a restaurant, eating, when suddenly one of them begins to look as if they are choking. Suddenly the entire restaurant is abuzz, and someone is always there who knows exactly how to respond to a choking victim. This person rushes to the table to save the day. One has to wonder how often this same scenario would play out if it were to occur in real life. What would happen if you were in that restaurant? Would you know how to respond in order to save someone's life? Unfortunately, the number of people who would know what to do is not as large as it should be. Now, let's take this scene a little bit further and imagine you were at home, all alone, when you began to choke. The sheer panic would be enough to stop someone from being able to think clearly. For many people in this situation, the outcome is devastating. However, for one woman named Debbie, not only was she able to think clearly herself, but she also had an unsuspected savior by her side; a golden retriever named Toby.

Toby was a typical two-year-old golden retriever. He was a happy and boisterous pet with little formal training under his belt. While Toby was a good dog, he suffered the same distraction and lack of focus that many playful pups experience until they reach an older age. He was loved, but he was also not the type of dog you would expect to step up and save the day with confident resolve.

On the fateful day that Toby gained his hero status, Debbie had been at home alone, just her and her dogs. She was enjoying an apple that was crisp, juicy, and delicious. While she was eating, a piece of the apple became lodged in her windpipe. The piece was large enough that it was interfering with her ability to breathe. Debbie thought quickly, and immediately began performing the Heimlich maneuver on herself.

The Heimlich maneuver is a specific method of applying abdominal thrusts when an object becomes lodged in a person's throat, blocking the airway. Without oxygen, brain damage can occur in as little as four to six minutes, with death following shortly after.

The Heimlich maneuver is done by placing your fist, thumb side in, just above the navel; with the other hand over it. You then apply upward thrusts in an effort to dislodge the stuck object. Debbie knew how to perform the Heimlich on herself, but after several attempts she remained unsuccessful. She then began pounding on her chest as fear began to sink in. While she was doing this, the last thing she was thinking about was that her dog Toby was there watching and paying very close attention to what was going on with her.

As she continued to pound on her chest, but was unable to breathe in any air, Toby decided that for the safety of his human, it was time for him act. Before Debbie even knew it, Toby had knocked her to the floor, and standing above her, placed his paws on her chest and began jumping up and down. Take a moment to revisit the part of Toby's story where we mention that Toby was in no way the most trained of dogs. He had no official obedience training, no medical rescue dog training, no real reason to observe and copy what Debbie was doing at that moment. But he did. He recognized that Debbie was in trouble, and observed what she was trying to do to save herself. When she was unable to do, it jumped in and did it himself.

After a few of Toby's jumps the apple was dislodged from Debbie's throat. As soon as the apple came up out of her windpipe Toby knew to stop the Heimlich, and then immediately turned his efforts into keeping Debbie from passing out by lavishly licking her face. Debbie went to the doctor, with paw shaped bruises on her chest and was told that if it weren't for Toby jumping in to save her that there was a very good chance that she would not be here today to tell the story of her miraculous dog.

Sometimes you may hear detractors say it is impossible for a dog to really understand a human, or to communicate and interact with us on the same level. Toby's heroic story says otherwise. It was as if Debbie was describing to him what needed to be done with her actions. He immediately recognized that her life was in danger and he wasted no time in jumping in to save her. He knew when to stop, and he knew that he also needed to help keep her conscious. How can we explain all of this, if we disregard the depth of the relationship between dog and mankind?

Choking is the fourth leading cause of unintentional death from injury. In 2013 approximately 4,800 people died from choking in the United States. Food is the number one culprit in adults, especially for the elderly or for people who have dentures or other dental devices which may interfere with the ability to properly chew food. Young children are also at great risk due to the small objects they tend to put in their mouths. While many people know the Heimlich maneuver and unresponsive CPR, the number should be greater to prevent and rescue the thousands of people the choke every year. Debbie was extremely lucky that Toby was by her side that day. Even she, who knew what she was doing, would have become a choking fatality that day, if it weren't for one loving Golden Retriever.

Toby became an overnight celebrity in the following days after saving Debbie's life. With invitations to major network news and talk shows and countless requests for interviews, soon Toby's story was being told around the world and around the internet. Who can blame people for wanting to spread the word of this beautiful and loving dog?

Parting Words

There are few connections more powerful than those between man and dog. There are cat people, there are bird people, there are people who just don't care for any type of animal, and then there are dog people. You hear pet owners recounting stories of special connections between them and their beloved companion, and the most powerful of those stories always seem to come from those who speak of their experiences with the canine world.

Dogs understand us on a level that is difficult to comprehend. They learn our verbal and physical language and can respond to a simple action, or even just a glance. Dogs each have a unique set of characteristics that not only makes them an individual, but guides the many ways they can influence and impact our lives.

The stories in this book are of some of the most amazing dog heroes today. Here you have read of both decorated war heroes and treasured pets. There are no social barriers when it comes to dog heroes. Breed, temperament, and age do not matter. From young to old, from well trained to not trained, each dog saved the lives of others, either physically or emotionally.

With these stories we can go forth with a lighter heart and little more hope for humanity, as long as we keep our faithful canine companions at our sides. I hope you have enjoyed these stories and they have filled your heart and lifted your spirits in the way that only a miracle dog can.

I can't thank you enough for purchasing my book and hope you enjoyed these true doc hero stories. If I can ask a favor, if you have time, please review my book on Amazon. That would be so awesome. Thank you.

Other Books by Lou Jefferson

To check it out, just click on the cover.

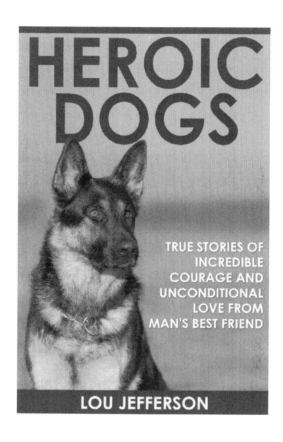

Made in the USA
San Bernardino, CA
14 December 2016

True dog stories that will inspire and warm yo[ur] heart. These incredible dog heroes ha[ve] demonstrated acts of bravery, courage, a[nd] intelligence beyond and above what you wou[ld] expect of man's best friend.